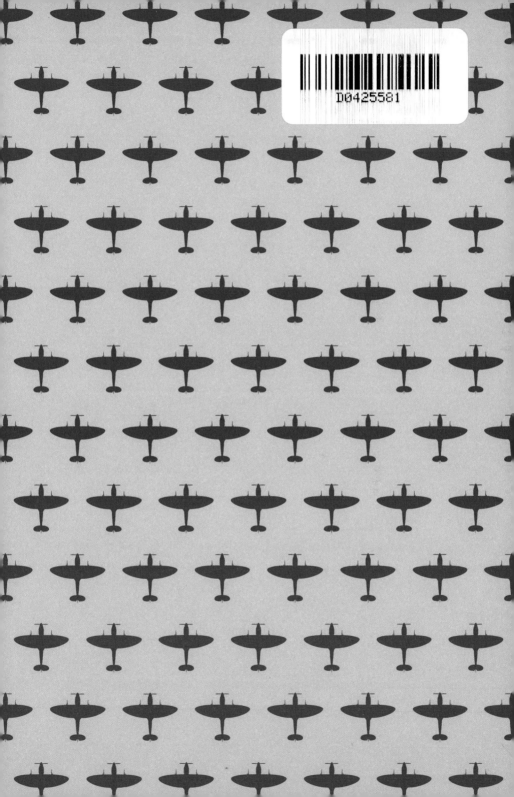

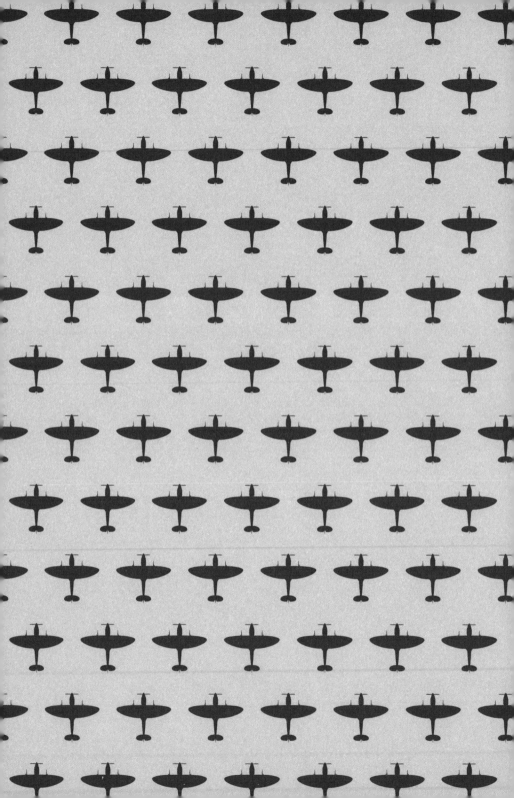

BIOGRAPHIC
CHURCHILL

BIOGRAPHIC
CHURCHILL

RICHARD WILES

AMMONITE
PRESS

First published 2017 by
Ammonite Press
an imprint of Guild of Master Craftsman Publications Ltd
Castle Place, 166 High Street, Lewes, East Sussex, BN7 1XU,
United Kingdom

ISBN 978 1 78145 301 8

Publisher: Jason Hook
Concept Design: Matt Carr
Design & Illustration: Matt Carr & Robin Shields
Editor: Jamie Pumfrey
Consultant Editor: Jon Cooksey

Colour reproduction by GMC Reprographics
Printed and bound in Turkey

Picture credits:
15: Shutterstock/Everett-Art; 24: Shutterstock/Alexander
Smulskiy; 25: Shutterstock/Vitezslav Halamka; 28: Getty
Images/ Universal Images Group; 33: iStock/Elenabs; 44:
Shutterstock/Basel101658; 52: Shutterstock/MapensStudio;
56: Shutterstock/Shaineast; 72: iStock/Djvstock; 74:
Shutterstock/ Peteri; 82: Shutterstock/Boreala.

CONTENTS

ICONOGRAPHIC

WHEN WE CAN RECOGNIZE A POLITICIAN BY A SET OF ICONS, WE CAN ALSO RECOGNIZE HOW COMPLETELY THAT POLITICIAN AND THEIR STORY HAVE ENTERED OUR CULTURE AND OUR CONSCIOUSNESS.

INTRODUCTION

Historian, war correspondent, artist, writer of more than 40 books, bricklayer, inveterate hat wearer, designer of the adult romper suit, ardent smoker of Havana cigars and a man with a passion for the fizz of champagne: a diverse collection of activities for any one person. But the expansive personality and interests of Sir Winston Spencer-Churchill – the British statesman who served as prime minister in 1940–45 and again in 1951–55 – cannot be contained neatly within a single category. He was, indeed, a man of many parts.

Born in 1874 into a titled family, with a long and noteworthy pedigree, Winston enjoyed a comparatively privileged upbringing. However, as is often the case with noble stock, he did not have inexaustible wealth. Although rationed in his parents' affections, he found solace in the company of his childhood nanny. He was an awkward child with little ability or interest in academic success. At his three public schools, he did show prowess on the playing field but his poor academic record was partly due to rebelliousness and his aversion to learning the classics.

"I WOULD FAR RATHER HAVE BEEN APPRENTICED AS A BRICKLAYER'S MATE, OR RUN ERRANDS AS A MESSENGER BOY, OR HELPED MY FATHER TO DRESS THE FRONT WINDOWS OF A GROCER'S SHOP. IT WOULD HAVE BEEN REAL."

After leaving school, Churchill entered military college, where he excelled and was commissioned into the 4th Queen's Own Hussars. It was while stationed as a subaltern in India that he developed a voracious appetite for reading and a talent for writing. Devouring works on history, religion and politics by the likes of Edward Gibbon, Thomas Babington Macaulay and William Winwood Reade, and writing critiques of parliamentary debate, his command of the English language blossomed.

In Hyderabad in 1899, aged 25, he met the first significant love of his life, society beauty Pamela Plowden, daughter of civil servant Sir Trevor Chichele-Plowden. His proposal of marriage was rebuffed on account of his lack of money. In having to rely on the inadequate financial support of his mother, Churchill discovered a means to supplement his allowance by selling his services to newspapers as a war correspondent. In return for rousing front-line reports from various theatres of war, which enthralled readers, he could command huge sums of money.

In 1908, Churchill became reacquainted with Clementine Hozier, the woman with whom he would thereafter enjoy a lifelong romance. After a brief courtship, they married the same year. Children followed rapidly, first Diana, then Randolph, Sarah, Marigold, who sadly died from septicaemia at the age of three, and finally Mary.

Churchill first dipped his toes in the waters of politics in the Oldham by-election of 1899. Failing to win the seat, he returned to reporting on the Boer conflict, during which he was captured and made a prisoner of war. After a daring escape, he returned to England a hero. Standing for Parliament again in the 1900 general election, he won the Oldham seat, and so commenced a 50-year career in politics that would take him through many important cabinet posts to the pinnacle, as prime minister.

He was, at times, a controversial figure – notably in the case of the disastrous Gallipoli landings during the First World War – and he was not without his detractors. Churchill remained outspoken in matters he felt passionate about. But it was in the Second World War that he left his most indelible mark and gained the affections and respect of a nation in peril. His carefully sculpted speeches and radio broadcasts, delivered with exquisite precision, were a beacon of light, a defiant stance against the tyranny of Nazi Germany.

With his physical and mental health declining in the mid-1950s, a series of strokes brought about his resignation. He spent his twilight years at Chartwell, Kent, in the company of his loyal wife. Even in the 1960s he tried to remain active in public life, but a severe stroke in 1965 preceded his death at the age of 90. Honoured with a state funeral, Sir Winston Churchill took his place in history, and is remembered by many as one of the greatest Britons.

Even after the war, no longer prime minister but leader of the opposition, Churchill continued to influence world affairs, delivering the first shot across the bows in the Cold War. Returning to government as prime minister in 1951, at the age of 77, he championed a massive effort in building hundreds of thousands of new homes. On the international stage he attempted to maintain Britain's 'special relationship' with the United States, while in colonial matters he battled to retain what he could of the British Empire.

WINSTON CHURCHILL

01
LIFE

"NEVER GIVE IN – NEVER, NEVER, NEVER, IN NOTHING GREAT OR SMALL, LARGE OR PETTY, NEVER GIVE IN EXCEPT TO CONVICTIONS OF HONOUR AND GOOD SENSE. NEVER YIELD TO FORCE; NEVER YIELD TO THE APPARENTLY OVERWHELMING MIGHT OF THE ENEMY."

—Winston Churchill, in a speech at Harrow School, 29 October 1941

WINSTON LEONARD SPENCER-CHURCHILL

was born on 30 November 1874 at Blenheim Palace, Woodstock, Oxfordshire, ancestral home of the Dukes of Marlborough.

WOODSTOCK

OXFORDSHIRE

Winston Leonard Spencer-Churchill was the first son of Lord Randolph Churchill and his American wife, the socialite Jeanette 'Jennie' Jerome. A politician and chancellor of the exchequer, Randolph was descended from the aristocratic Spencer family (which would include Diana, the Princess of Wales), while Jennie was the daughter of an American millionaire.

The family, who lived on Charles Street, in Mayfair, London, had been attending a St Andrew's Ball at Blenheim. According to a letter written by Randolph, his wife fell while out walking with shooters, followed by a rough ride in a pony carriage, which brought on labour pains. His son was delivered by the local country doctor eight hours later, at 1.30 in the morning. It is possible that, rather than being born two months prematurely, Churchill was conceived before his parents' marriage, less than eight months before.

UNITED KINGDOM

Another famous ▶
inhabitant of Woodstock:
Elizabeth I (1533–1603)
who was imprisoned at
Woodstock Palace by her
sister, Queen Mary I

UNITED STATES

American businessman Joseph F. Glidden receives patent for barbed wire after lengthy legal dispute.

GREAT BRITAIN

Benjamin Disraeli succeeds William Gladstone as British prime minister.

UNITED STATES

In Texas, a force of 600 soldiers raid the last sanctuary of the Kiowa, Comanche and Cheyenne Indian tribes, forcibly removing them to designated reserves in Oklahoma.

GREAT BRITAIN

Following trials in London, the General Post Office announces that red will replace the green colour formerly used on all pillar and post boxes.

THE WORLD IN 1874

RUSSIA

Prince Alfred, Duke of Edinburgh, second son of Queen Victoria and Prince Albert of Saxe-Coburg and Gotha, marries Grand Duchess Maria Alexandrovna, daughter of Emperor Alexander II of Russia. She is the only member of the Romanov dynasty to marry into the British royal family. Her Majesty is not amused.

FRANCE

Louis Leroy, writing in *Le Charivari*, criticizes the first exhibition of paintings by Monet, Pissarro, Sisley and Renoir, coining the term 'Impressionists' with reference to Monet's *Impression, Sunrise*, which the group subsequently adopts.

AUSTRIA

Franz Hoyer establishes a workshop in Schönbach (now part of the Czech Republic), a town famous for its muscial instrument production. The Hoyer family made lutes and zithers before changing to classical, folk and eventually electric guitars.

INDIA

The first horse-drawn bus is introduced on the streets of Mumbai, India, by the Bombay Tramway Company, serving two routes.

WINSTON'S FAMILY

Despite growing up with social status and privilege, Winston's immediate family had relatively little money; his father, Lord Randolph Churchill, as the third son of John Winston Spencer-Churchill, 7th Duke of Marlborough, did not inherit a title or property. His mother, Jennie Jerome, was the second of four daughters of American millionaire Leonard Jerome.

ROYAL CONNECTIONS

Sir Winston Churchill and Lady Diana Spencer were fourth cousins, two times removed. Their lineage stems from John Churchill, 1st Duke of Marlborough (1650–1722) and his wife Sarah Jennings. Winston's family tree branches from their eldest daughter Henrietta, great grandmother of George Spencer-Churchill, 5th Duke of Marlborough. Princess Diana was an ancestor of their second daughter, Anne, who married Charles Spencer, 3rd Earl of Sunderland (1675–1722).

5th Duke of Marlborough
George Spencer-Churchill
(1766–1840)

6th Duke of Marlborough
George Spencer-Churchill
(1793–1857)

One of 4 siblings

One of 11 siblings

Clementine O. Hozier
(1885–1977)

Sir Winston Leonard Spencer-Churchill
(1874–1965)

Diana Churchill
(1909–63)

Randolph F.E. Churchill
(1911–68)

Susan Stewart
(1767–1841)

(1st Wife)
Lady Jane Stewart
(1798–1844)

1st
Cousins

7th Duke of Marlborough
John Winston
Spencer-Churchill
(1822–83)

Frances Anne
Vane
(1822–99)

Randolph Henry
Spencer-Churchill
(1849–95)

Jeanette 'Jennie'
Jerome
(1854–1921)

John Strange
Spencer-Churchill
(1880–1947)

Sarah M.H.
Churchill
(1914–82)

Marigold F.
Churchill
(1918–21)

Mary Spencer-
Churchill
(1922–2014)

YOUNG WINSTON

As was the norm in the social class of Churchill's parents, child-rearing was the domain of nannies, leaving the parents free to pursue a whirl of social engagements and infidelities. It was a lonely life for a sensitive child, and Winston formed a strong bond with his nanny, Mrs Elizabeth Ann Everest, whom he affectionately addressed as 'Woom' or 'Woomany'. Churchill's schooldays were unhappy. Regarded by his tutors as rebellious, backward and precocious, he hated formal education and consequently performed poorly, other than in subjects – such as geography and English – that inspired him.

At the tender age of seven, Winston was sent to board at St George's, Ascot, whose pupils invariably graduated to Eton. It boasted classes of only 10 boys, electric lights, a swimming pool and sports grounds.

JUST DESSERTS

At St George's School, Winston once kicked the headmaster's straw hat to pieces in a fit of fury, after being caned for stealing sugar.

1876 1877 1878 1879 1880 1881 1882 1883 1884

From the age of two until five, Winston lived with his family in Dublin, Ireland, where his father was private secretary to his grandfather, John Spencer-Churchill, the Viceroy.

Winston, whose health suffered during his time at St George's, was removed after two years, on the suggestion of the family doctor. He completed his elementary education boarding in the more sympathetic environment of Brunswick School in Hove, Sussex.

NURSERY TIMES

Before he was wrenched from the arms of his nanny and packed off to boarding school, Winston adored his nursery. Favourite playthings included a real steam engine, a magic lantern and an army of nearly 1,000 toy soldiers.

'COPPERKNOB'

During his Harrow years, Winston was a stocky lad with red hair, and irreverently nicknamed 'copperknob' by his peers.

Enrolled at Harrow School with lamentably poor entrance exam scores, Winston suffered the humiliation of being placed bottom of the bottom class, much to his father's disgust. Unwilling to apply himself to studying the classics, he excelled at history and geography, and developed a love of the English language.

BEGGING LETTERS

Despite writing letters begging his mother to visit him at school, or to allow him to come home during holidays, she rarely visited him. His relationship with his revered father, who was disappointed in his son's poor academic progress, became distant.

1886 1887 1888 1889 1890 1891 1892 1893

EN GARDE!

Winston demonstrated considerable skill with an épée, winning a Public Schools Championship. His opponents reportedly fell victim to his nimble footwork and dashing attack.

Winston left Harrow intent on a career in the military, but his weak academic abilities meant he only just scraped through the entrance examinations for Sandhurst Royal Military College, Berkshire, after three attempts. His lack of qualifications gained him admittance to the cavalry, but not the infantry as his father had hoped.

STAMPS OF THE WORLD

As a boy Winston avidly collected postage stamps from all over the world, many given to him by his father. His own image was later to grace a series of commemorative stamps.

4d

A DEFINING YEAR

The year 1895 marked a dramatic turning point in Churchill's life. After a troubled and lonely childhood he came of age as a confident and calculating young man with a clear vision of his future.

OFFICER AND GENTLEMAN

The environment of Sandhurst enthused Churchill and he became an adept horseman. Graduating in December 1894, he was commissioned as a second lieutenant in the 4th Queen's Own Hussars on 20 February.

FATHER FIGURE

Despite a somewhat distant relationship, Churchill revered his charismatic father, and dreamed of entering Parliament at his side. His hope was dashed when Lord Randolph died on 24 January at the age of just 45.

CUBAN ZEAL!

Churchill travelled to Cuba to observe the Cuban War of Independence. During his time there, he discovered the pleasures of smoking Havana cigars, a habit that would remain with him for the rest of his life.

NANNY DEAREST

While stationed at Aldershot, Churchill received word that his nanny, Mrs Everest, was dying, and rushed to be with her at her sister's house in North London, where she was staying. She died of peritonitis while her former charge sat at her bedside. He later wrote in *My Early Life*:

"SHE HAD BEEN MY DEAREST AND MOST INTIMATE FRIEND DURING THE WHOLE OF THE 20 YEARS I HAD LIVED."

THEATRES OF WAR

Winston found his stride in the cavalry, and excelled at horse riding. Craving action – and believing a military career to be the perfect preparation for a life in politics – he used his mother's connections to get himself posted to various battlefronts.

1895 CUBAN WAR OF INDEPENDENCE

Churchill got himself posted to Cuba, ostensibly to observe the Spanish Army fight against the insurgent Cuban guerrillas. He remained there for just three weeks.

1898 SUDAN

Attached to the 21st Lancers in Egypt, Churchill took part in the famous cavalry charge at the Battle of Omdurman in Sudan.

1896 INDIA

Transferred first to Bombay, then to Bangalore, Churchill was comfortably housed and spent his time educating himself with opinions that would colour his career.

1899 SOUTH AFRICA

Churchill resigned from the British Army, bent on pursuing a career as a writer and politician. Failing to win in the Oldham by-election, he travelled to South Africa to report on the Boer War for *The Morning Post*.

1897 NORTH-WEST FRONTIER

Churchill saw action during the Mohmand Campaign of 1897–8. As part of a 'search and destroy' mission in the Mamund valley, he came under heavy fire.

The Morning Post

1915–16 WESTERN FRONT

Churchill resigned from government and rejoined the British Army. As a lieutenant colonel commanding the 6th Battalion, Royal Scots Fusiliers, from January 1916, he was stationed at Ploegsteert in Belgium.

1900–05 ENGLAND

Churchill retired from the regular army in 1900 and, in 1901, volunteered in the Imperial Yeomanry as a Captain in the Queen's Own Oxfordshire Hussars. After being promoted to major in 1905, he took command of the Henley Squadron.

1916 TERRITORIAL FORCE

Churchill transferred to the Territorial Force Reserve of officers.

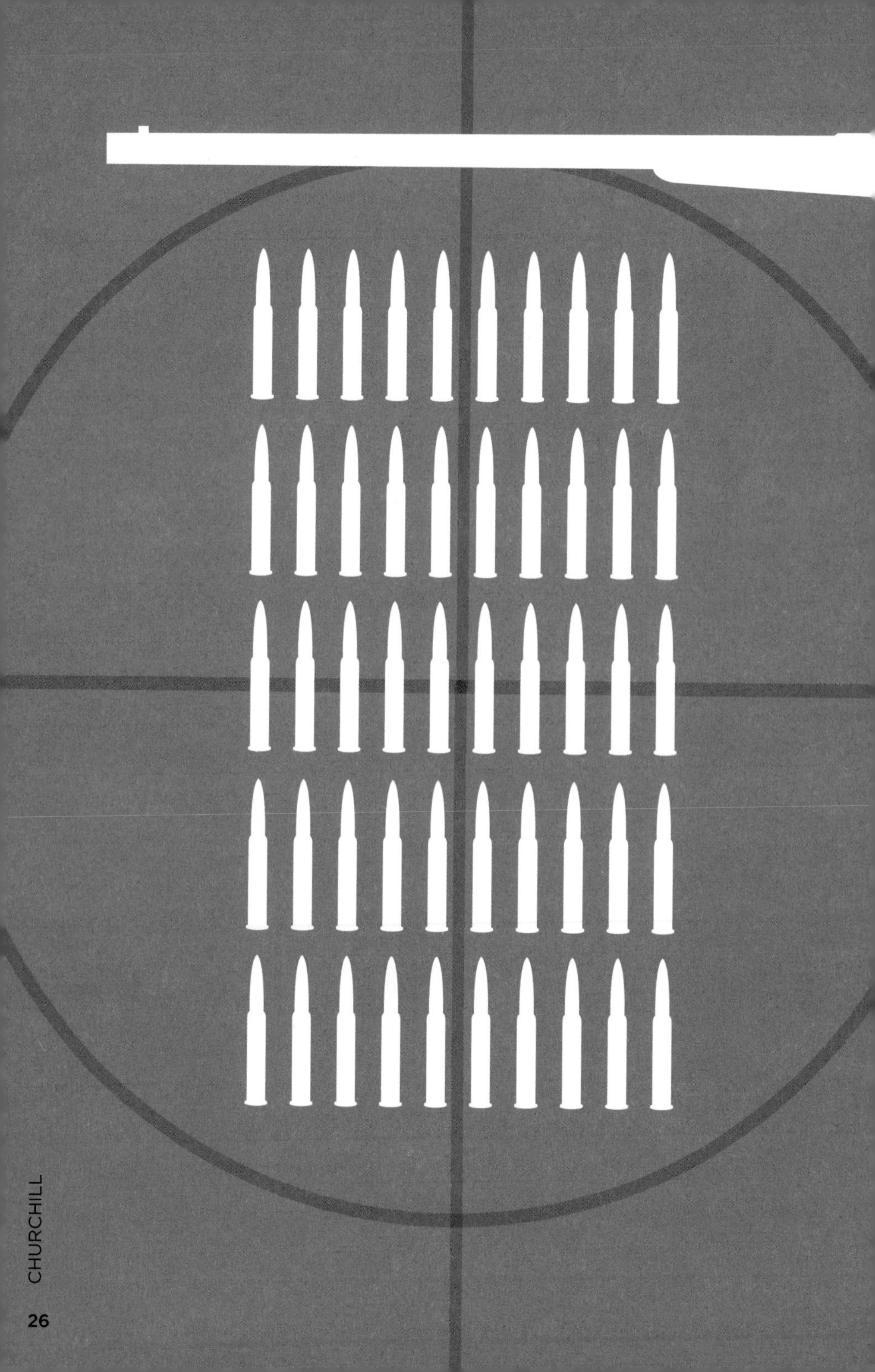

CHURCHILL WAS SHOT AT OVER 50 TIMES

Winston first came under enemy fire on his 21st birthday, trekking with Spanish troops to Arroyo Blanco, Cuba, when they encountered forces led by Major General Máximo Gómez. Two years later he saw combat on the North-West Frontier against an uprising of Afghan tribes fighting British rule, when, despite the British advantage of the newly introduced Maxim machine gun, the enemy were able to get close enough to fire on the British and Indian troops. On the Western Front in 1916, during his command of the 6th Royal Scots Fusiliers battalion, he made 36 night-time forays to the shell craters of no-man's land, a few feet from the Germans, coming under machine-gun fire. A fellow soldier said, "He never fell when a shell went off; he never ducked when a bullet went past with its loud crack. He used to say, after watching me duck: 'It's no damn use ducking; the bullet has gone a long way past you by now.'"

WINNIE'S GREAT ESCAPE!

14 OCTOBER 1899

The Second Boer War between Britain and the Boer Republics rages. Churchill grasps an opportunity for self-promotion! Securing a commission as reporter for *The Morning Post*, he sails for South Africa ...

AMBUSHED

During his first assignment on a scouting expedition, the armoured train he's travelling on with a troop of British soldiers is ambushed by heavily armed Boers, having placed a boulder on the track. With disregard for his own safety, Winston supervises the soldiers to uncouple the derailed trucks so the locomotive can be used to shield them as they retreat back up the line.

OUTNUMBERED

Outnumbered, the soldiers surrender and are taken to Pretoria as prisoners of war. Winston's protestations that he is a civilian are to no avail.

500 number of heavily armed enemy Boers

WINSTON CHURCHILL, RIGHT, WITH OTHER CAPTURED PRISONERS OF WAR

ESCAPE

After two weeks in the prisoner of war camp – a converted school – wily Winnie scales a wall while the guards' backs are turned and escapes!

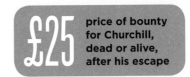

£25 price of bounty for Churchill, dead or alive, after his escape

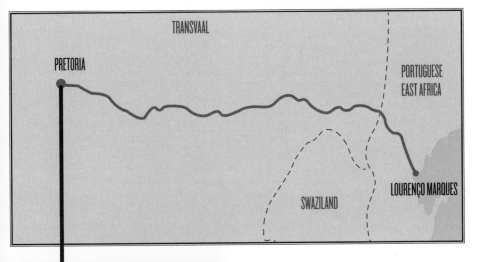

TRANSVAAL

PRETORIA

PORTUGUESE EAST AFRICA

LOURENÇO MARQUES

SWAZILAND

NIGHT TRAIN

Travelling by night to evade recapture, and stowing away on supply trains, he travels nearly 300 miles (500 kilometres) in nine days to reach Portuguese East Africa.

RETURNING HERO

Winston returns to South Africa a hero. The British press prints stirring accounts of his adventure. His celebrity assures his demand as a public speaker and proves crucial in launching his career in politics.

It's later claimed – not least by Churchill himself – that the Boer officer to whom he had surrendered at gunpoint was none other than General Louis Botha, future prime minister of the Union of South Africa (1910–19), who would become a close friend.

A CAREER IN POLITICS

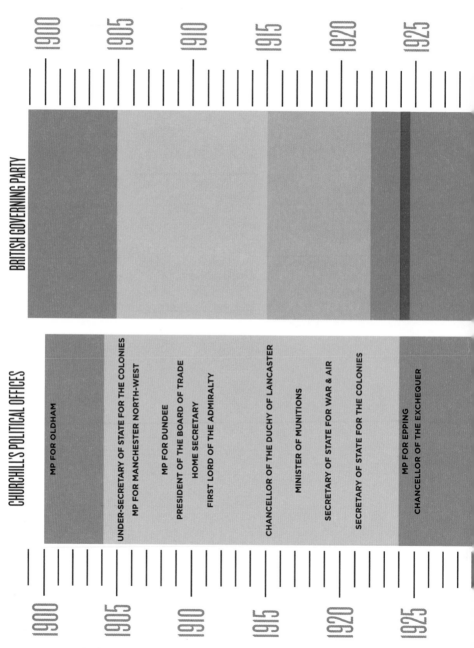

1900 1905 1910 1915 1920 1925

BRITISH GOVERNING PARTY

CHURCHILL'S POLITICAL OFFICES

MP FOR OLDHAM

UNDER-SECRETARY OF STATE FOR THE COLONIES

MP FOR MANCHESTER NORTH-WEST

MP FOR DUNDEE

PRESIDENT OF THE BOARD OF TRADE

HOME SECRETARY

FIRST LORD OF THE ADMIRALTY

CHANCELLOR OF THE DUCHY OF LANCASTER

MINISTER OF MUNITIONS

SECRETARY OF STATE FOR WAR & AIR

SECRETARY OF STATE FOR THE COLONIES

MP FOR EPPING

CHANCELLOR OF THE EXCHEQUER

1900 1905 1910 1915 1920 1925

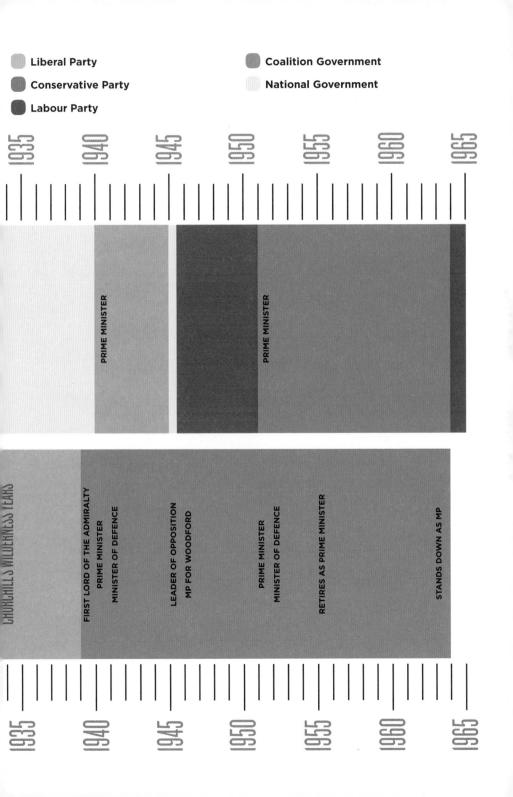

Liberal Party

Conservative Party

Labour Party

Coalition Government

National Government

1935　1940　1945　1950　1955　1960　1965

PRIME MINISTER

PRIME MINISTER

CHURCHILL'S WILDERNESS YEARS

FIRST LORD OF THE ADMIRALTY

PRIME MINISTER

MINISTER OF DEFENCE

LEADER OF OPPOSITION

MP FOR WOODFORD

PRIME MINISTER

MINISTER OF DEFENCE

RETIRES AS PRIME MINISTER

STANDS DOWN AS MP

1935　1940　1945　1950　1955　1960　1965

THE TROUBLE WITH WINSTON

Many of Churchill's ailments resulted from his accident-prone tendency, although in later life the strain of his responsibilities as prime minister undoubtedly contributed to his decline in physical and mental health. While holidaying in the south of France in the summer of 1949, he suffered a mild stroke, followed by a second in 1953 at 10 Downing Street. Despite partial paralysis down one side, he held a cabinet meeting the next morning. After retiring as prime minister in 1955 he suffered another mild stroke in December 1956.

1893 Nineteen-year-old Winston fell 29ft (9m) from a bridge into a tree when cavorting with friends, resulting in him being bedridden for three months with a RUPTURED KIDNEY.

1895 Winston received a KNEE INJURY when steeplechasing. Like most keen horsemen, he was prone to take many a tumble from the saddle.

1896 Disembarking a troop ship in Bombay, India, he tore the CAPSULAR ATTACHMENTS to his right shoulder joint. This injury caused persistent instability for the rest of his life, leading to dislocations at various times.

1899 Slipping on stone steps prior to competing in the Inter-Regimental Polo Tournament in Meerut, India, Churchill suffered a DISLOCATED SHOULDER and SPRAINED ANKLE. But he proceeded to score three goals – helping his team win the final – with his right elbow strapped to his torso.

1919 When learning to fly, he crashed his biplane and received a minor injury.

1921 Suffered a SEVERELY GRAZED WRIST after being unseated from a camel while visiting the Sphinx at Giza in Egypt in the company of Lawrence of Arabia.

1922
After suffering a pain attributed to indigestion for nearly a week, Winston was diagnosed with ACUTE APPENDICITIS. Due to the urgent need for an appendectomy, he was unable to travel to Dundee to defend his seat in the general election.

1931
Hit by a car while looking the wrong way, when crossing New York's Fifth Avenue, Churchill was hospitalized for a week with an INJURED FOREHEAD (causing a permanent scar) and THIGHS, resulting in PLEURISY.

1941
While staying at the White House just after the Japanese attack on Pearl Harbor, he suffered his first HEART ATTACK.

1943
Churchill became ill with a bacterial PNEUMONIA infection in the Near East and was treated with 'M&B', otherwise known as sulfadiazine, produced by May & Baker Pharmaceuticals.

1946
Churchill consulted Sir Alexander Fleming about a STAPHYLOCOCCAL INFECTION that had proved resistant to penicillin.

1949–63
Churchill suffered...
10 STROKES

1949–63
INCREASING DEAFNESS

1962
Eighty-seven-year-old Winston fell from his bed during a holiday in Monaco, FRACTURING HIS HIP. He then contracted BRONCHITIS and PNEUMONIA, followed by a THROMBOSIS.

DEATH OF A STATESMAN

Having survived several strokes over a 14-year period, increasingly deaf and with a deteriorating mental capacity, the grand old statesman died at his London home on the morning of Sunday 24 January 1965 at the age of 90. It was 70 years to the day after his father's death.

After lying in state in Westminster Hall before a funeral service in St Paul's Cathedral, Churchill was buried in the family plot at St Martin's Church, Bladon, not far from his birthplace at Blenheim.

His tombstone was replaced in 1998 and restored again in 2006, after the consistently heavy volume of visitors had caused serious erosion.

"I AM READY TO MEET MY MAKER. WHETHER MY MAKER IS PREPARED FOR THE GREAT ORDEAL OF MEETING ME IS ANOTHER MATTER."

WINSTON CHURCHILL

02
WORLD

"POLITICS ARE ALMOST AS EXCITING AS WAR, AND QUITE AS DANGEROUS ... IN WAR, YOU CAN ONLY BE KILLED ONCE, BUT IN POLITICS, MANY TIMES."

—Winston Churchill in conversation with author and journalist
Harold Begbie, cited in *Master Workers*, 1906

THE DEMON DRINK

Churchill was never far from an alcoholic beverage, and never shy to underplay the myth of his prodigious intake. He claimed that he had initially disliked whisky, but as a subaltern in India, where the water was unfit for drinking, whisky was added to make it palatable and, with perseverance, he developed a taste for it. In a typical day he might consume:

2 BOTTLES OF CHAMPAGNE

Winston adored champers – particularly Pol Roger – and would consume a pint-sized bottle at lunchtime and one with dinner, invariably out of a silver tankard.

2 BRANDIES

Churchill liked to take a cognac – preferably Hine – after his lunch, before retiring for a siesta. Another cognac would aid postprandial digestion in the evening.

1 GLASS OF SHERRY

A fine amontillado would sharpen Churchill's appetite for dinner, before he turned his attention to the second bottle of Champagne.

6 WHISKIES

Starting around 9.30am, he'd sip, not a single malt, but a blended whisky: a trickle of Johnny Walker Red Label in the bottom of a glass, topped up with soda water. He called this tipple his 'mouthwash'.

09:30 START

On a trip to the United States in 1932, during Prohibition, Churchill had to hand over a 'prescription' from Otto C. Pickhardt MD explaining that 'post-accident convalescence' necessitated the taking of alcoholic spirits. Of unspecified dosage, the minimum requirement was 8.5 fl oz (250ml), equating to 10 shots, or a 25 fl oz (750ml) bottle of spirits a day.

OTHER DRINKS WERE CONSUMED ACCORDING TO THE OCCASION, AND IN INDETERMINATE QUANTITIES:

MARTINI
As an aperitif – consisting of neat gin poured over ice, with a nod towards occupied France.

CLARET
Bottles of the dry red wine were always present during meals, and often mixed with soda.

NIGHTCAP
Churchill's final drink of the day – a fine port or a 90-year-old brandy – would be taken at around 10pm, after which he would complete another four hours' work before retiring to bed.

WAR AND BOOZE

In 1899, 25-year-old Churchill set off for the Boer War as a correspondent for *The Morning Post*, with supplies that no aristocratic English gentleman could be expected to survive without:

36 BOTTLES OF WINE AND PORT
18 BOTTLES OF 10-YEAR-OLD SCOTCH WHISKY
6 BOTTLES OF FRENCH VERMOUTH

WORLD

PEN FOR HIRE

In 1895, as a young cavalry officer, Churchill's annual salary was £121, the equivalent of £14,500 today. Added to that he received £500 (the equivalent of £59,000) from his mother every year, paid quarterly. Despite this, he frequently overspent.

Calculating that he would still need considerably more earnings, he guilefully mapped out a career path unreliant upon traditional promotion through the army ranks. He used his mother's influence in society to arrange postings to campaigns where he would be exposed to military action – where he could supplement his income as a war correspondent for several London newspapers.

WAR CORRESPONDENT

£250
PER MONTH
PLUS EXPENSES

Equivalent to

£29,250
today

ARMY WAGES

£10
PER MONTH

Equivalent to

£1,200
today

ALLOWANCE

£41
PER MONTH

Equivalent to

£4,900
today

CUBA

Although in Cuba for just three weeks, Churchill wrote about his exploits in reports commissioned by the *Daily Graphic*. Here he learned the basics of political analysis, military strategy and liaison with a foreign army.

NORTH-WEST FRONTIER

Churchill's articles were published in the Indian newspaper *The Allahabad Pioneer* and *The Daily Telegraph*, while in late 1897 he also found time to pen his first book, *The Story of the Malakand Field Force*.

SUDAN

While serving in Sudan in 1898, Churchill sent dispatches to *The Morning Post*, later writing about the Mahdist War in his work *The River War*, published in two volumes in 1899.

SOUTH AFRICA

In 1899 Churchill was commissioned as war correspondent for *The Morning Post*, and the following year published his book *London to Ladysmith via Pretoria*, an account of his experiences during the Second Anglo-Boer War and his capture and imprisonment. The subject of the conflict was continued in *Ian Hamilton's March*.

Why did he command such high earnings for his writing?

His dispatches, written in the style of vivid, graphic, frequently bloody adventure stories, made compelling reading, and helped to boost the circulation of the papers.

THE TEETH THAT HELPED WIN THE WAR

People with speech impediments often make efforts to conceal or eradicate them, and as a young man Winston, who had a similar impediment to his father, sought specialist help. Practice and perseverance was prescribed. In later life, however, he went to considerable lengths to actually retain the lateral lisp – in which 's' and 'z' sounds are produced with airflow over the sides of the tongue instead of the front – that had become the most recognizable characteristic of his wartime radio broadcasts.

At the start of the Second World War, young dental technician Derek Cudlipp made four customized sets of upper dentures for Churchill, which did not connect fully with the roof of the mouth, and consequently preserved his distinctive lisp. Churchill carried a spare set with him at all times.

£15,200

NATIONAL SERVICE

When Cudlipp's call-up papers arrived, Churchill tore them up, saying that the technician would be more important to the war effort if he stayed in London to repair his dentures rather than joining up to fight. Since Churchill was apt to flick out his dentures when angry and toss them across the room, his decision seems well founded.

A SET OF CHURCHILL'S DENTURES SOLD AT AUCTION IN 2010 FOR £15,200 – THREE TIMES THEIR ESTIMATE – TO A BRITISH COLLECTOR OF CHURCHILL MEMORABILIA.

"MY IMPEDIMENT IS NO HINDRANCE"

—Churchill, in reference to his lisp

THE KING'S SPEECH

A contemporary of Churchill who sought to conquer his speech impediment, rather than capitalize on it, was newly crowned King George VI. Tutored by Australian speech and language therapist Lionel Logue, he overcame a stammer to make his first wartime radio broadcast on Britain's declaration of war with Germany in 1939.

THE BLACK DOG

Although Churchill may not have suffered from clinical depression, he was prone to bouts of apprehension, anxiety and despair. During his darker periods he would experience lethargy, loss of appetite and lack of concentration, sometimes taking to his bed. After a few months he would emerge re-energized, typically staying up until the early hours of the morning dictating books and writing speeches.

He referred to such periods of depression as his 'black dog', a term first used by English writer Samuel Johnson in the 1780s to describe his own condition. In a letter to Clementine in 1911, Churchill cited a friend's wife, who was treated for depression by a German doctor: "I think this man might be useful to me – if my black dog returns. He seems quite away from me now – it is such a relief. All the colours come back into the picture."

Churchill did not take medication for depression – although it has been suggested that his heavy drinking was a form of self-medication – but amphetamine was prescribed to help with important speeches and events after his stroke in 1953. However, Churchill understood that worry and mental strain were inherent in a position of exceptional responsibility such as his, and wrote about this in *Painting as a Pastime*. His hobbies – painting and bricklaying – served to diffuse his stresses.

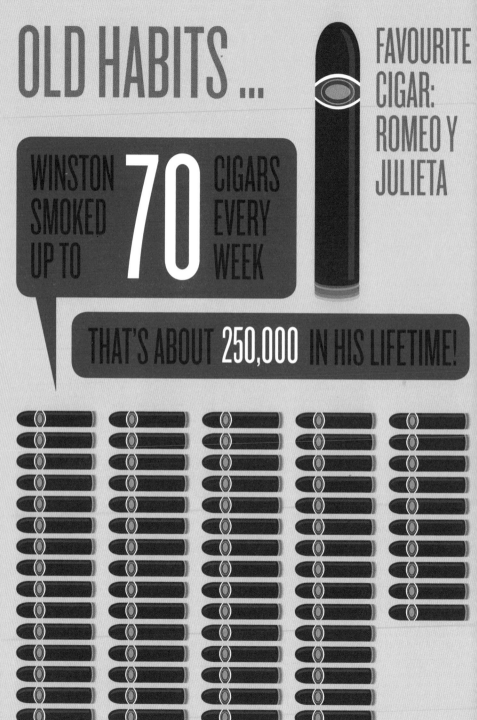

OLD HABITS ...

FAVOURITE CIGAR: ROMEO Y JULIETA

WINSTON SMOKED UP TO **70** CIGARS EVERY WEEK

THAT'S ABOUT **250,000** IN HIS LIFETIME!

HOW DOES THIS COMPARE TO TWO OTHER GREAT CIGAR SMOKERS?

GEORGE BURNS
105 CIGARS A WEEK

PIPE DREAM

Churchill rarely finished a cigar, according to valet Norman McGowan, who was charged with collecting the butts and giving them to Kearns, one of the gardeners at his country home Chartwell, to smoke in his pipe.

SIGMUND FREUD
140 CIGARS A WEEK

IMPRESSIONS OF WINSTON

Winston Churchill was an accomplished and sensitive amateur painter, after discovering the hobby at the age of 40 on resigning from government in 1915. In painting he found solace and escape from bouts of depression, and it was a passion that would endure for his lifetime.

Favouring oils over watercolours, he excelled at impressionistic landscapes and seascapes, although he also painted interiors and portraits. His mentor was Anglo-French artist, Paul Lucien Maze, whom he met in the trenches during the First World War, and who became a lifelong friend.

As with many artists, Churchill's paintings achieved modest prices in his lifetime, but rocketed in value after his death – although for Winston, art, unlike his writing, was never seen as a source of income.

1921

4 paintings, submitted for exhibition in Paris, sold for £30 each.

1947

2 paintings submitted under his pseudonym are accepted by The Royal Academy.

2011

£2.29m The price *The Tower of Katoubia Mosque*, given to US President Harry Truman, when put up for sale in the USA.

2015

On the death of Mary Soames, Churchill's last surviving child, 37 paintings are accepted for the nation in lieu of inheritance tax. The collection would have settled £9.4m of tax – more than was due – but executors for Soames waive the difference.

2014

The Goldfish Pool at Chartwell is sold at auction for £1.8 million.

£1.8m

CHURCHILL PRODUCED MORE THAN **500** PAINTINGS OVER **48** YEARS

CHURCHILL USED THE PSEUDONYMS 'CHARLES MORIN' AND 'MR WINTER', SO THAT HIS SKILL COULD BE JUDGED ON ITS ARTISTIC MERIT.

"WHEN I GET TO HEAVEN I MEAN TO SPEND A CONSIDERABLE PORTION OF MY FIRST MILLION YEARS IN PAINTING, AND SO GET TO THE BOTTOM OF THE SUBJECT ..."

—Winston Churchill, on his passion for painting, in *Thoughts and Adventures*, 1932

CLOTHES MAKETH THE MAN

Churchill cut a striking figure with his overcoat, homburg hat and ever-present Cuban cigar, but practicality and comfort were the main criteria in his somewhat unconventional wardrobe.

WINSTON'S ONESIE

Churchill invented the 'siren suit', a practical one-piece zip-up over-garment intended for wearing during air-raids. A cross between a boiler suit and a child's onesie, tailors Turnbull & Asser made several for him in different coloured velvets and other fabrics, including a smart pinstripe version. The garment was described by Churchill's children as his 'romper'.

SLIPPERS

After a hard day, Churchill would ease his feet into a customized-crested pair of slippers made for him by Hook, Knowles & Co.

TITFERS

Hats expressed Churchill's individuality, while many increased his height and made him conspicuous in crowds. Apart from official headgear – busbies, topees (C), silk top hats (D), cocked hats – worn on military and ceremonial occasions – he also possessed many stetsons (E), homburgs (B) and bowlers, including the tall-crowned Cambridge model he nicknamed the 'Bowker' (A).

BOW TIE

Churchill said he wore spotted bow ties in tribute to his distant father, in an attempt to please him.

SILK UNDIES

Winston's underwear, from the Army & Navy Stores, was made of finely woven silk, pale pink in colour, its softness vital, he stated, for the wellbeing of his delicate and sensitive skin. Silk, during wartime, was an extravagance, and "cost the eyes out of his head", according to his wife Clementine.

ASTRAKHAN OVERCOAT

Churchill was often seen wearing his distinctive four-buttoned, fleece-collared Astrakhan coat.

5 THINGS YOU DIDN'T KNOW ABOUT CHURCHILL

01 BRICK BY BRICK

Churchill was an accomplished bricklayer, and was a member of the Amalgamated Union of Building Trade Workers. He found the activity relaxing, and built several buildings and walls at Chartwell.

02 MINTED

Winston's image appeared on a 1965 crown, the first commoner to be placed on a British coin.

03 ALTITUDE PROBLEM

In an unpressurized aeroplane flying to Moscow in 1942, oxygen masks were issued to all passengers. Churchill had his adapted so that he could smoke his cigar while wearing it.

04 HONORARY CITIZEN

In 1963, President John F. Kennedy, acting under authorization of an Act of Congress, proclaimed Churchill the first honorary citizen of the United States. Although Churchill was unable to attend a ceremony at the White House, his son and grandson accepted the award on his behalf.

05 GAMBLING MAN

Churchill was an inveterate, yet unlucky, gambler who could not resist a flutter at the casinos. In the 1930s, while holidaying in the south of France, he would gamble so heavily that he frittered away the modern equivalent of about £40,000 each year.

WINSTON
CHURCHILL

03
WORK

"I FELT AS IF I WERE WALKING WITH DESTINY, AND THAT ALL MY PAST LIFE HAD BEEN BUT A PREPARATION FOR THIS HOUR AND FOR THIS TRIAL."

—Winston Churchill, on his appointment as prime minister on 10 May 1940, from *The Second World War, Vol. I: The Gathering Storm*, 1948

MAN ON THE MOVE

Churchill was an ambitious man of action. He was passionate about technology, particularly aviation, and a staunch advocate of modernizing. In the prelude to the First World War, during the conflict and in the post-war coalition that followed, he made his mark not only on government, but also on the future of the British Empire – although his pretensions as a military strategist were almost scuppered by the disastrous Gallipoli Campaign.

1917

Despite being critical of Churchill's political and personal motives, prime minister David Lloyd-George appoints him to the role of Minister of Munitions, which had been created in 1915 after a shortage of artillery shells for the front line.

1916

Resigning from government in 1915 after Gallipoli, Churchill rejoins the British Army intent on salvaging his tarnished reputation. He is appointed lieutenant colonel, commanding the 6th Royal Scots Fusiliers battalion, and is stationed at Ploegsteert, Belgium, on the Western Front.

1911

Appointed First Lord of the Admiralty in October 1911, Churchill champions the modernizing of the fleet, launching a programme to replace coal power with oil power in ships.

1913

Heavier-than-air flight is less than a decade old when Churchill climbs into the cockpit of a B.E.2a biplane to take flying lessons at the Central Flying School in Wiltshire.

1915

Financed by the Navy, Churchill establishes the Landships Committee in February, charged with developing armoured fighting vehicles for use on the Western Front. This eventually leads to the creation of the tank.

As one of the political and military architects of the Gallipoli landings, he receives much of the blame for the disastrous campaign, which results in the humiliating evacuation of all forces.

19

ppointed to the
ual offices of Secretary
f State for War and
ecretary of State for Air.
 August, at his suggestion,
 e 10-Year Rule comes into
ffect, a guideline allowing the
reasury to control strategic,
foreign and financial policies
provided that the British
Empire did not engage
in a great war within the
next decade.

Churchill sanctions the use
of tear gas in Iraq, although
it is not needed after
bombing proves effective.

1929

After the defeat of the
Conservative government
in the general election,
Churchill becomes
estranged from the
leadership over protective
tariffs and Indian Home
Rule, and enters his
'wilderness years'.

1924

Having rejoined the
Conservative Party,
Churchill, as Chancellor
of the Exchequer, presents
a budget he later regards
as the greatest error in his
life: a return to the pre-war
exchange rate and 'gold
standard', which depresses
industries, notably coal
and cotton, resulting in
deflation, unemployment,
the miners' strike and
subsequent General
Strike of 1926.

1920

An advocate of foreign
intervention, Churchill
prolongs Allied involvement
in the Russian Civil War
and, after the last British
forces are finally withdrawn,
arranges for arms to be
sent to the Poles to bolster
their invasion of Ukraine.

1921

Churchill's brainchild, the
paramilitary 'Black and
Tans' are sent to assist
the Royal Irish Constabulary
fight the Irish Republican Army
(IRA) during the Irish War of
Independence. As Secretary of
State for the Colonies, he is a
signatory of the Anglo-Irish
Treaty that establishes
the Irish Free State.

1923

As a paid consultant for
Burmah Oil, Churchill
successfully lobbies for the
company to have exclusive
rights to Persian (Iranian)
oil resources.

4 January, 1911

THE SIEGE OF SIDNEY STREET

200 POLICE

AND 21 ARMY MARKSMEN IN GUN BATTLE WITH 2 ARMED ANARCHISTS

A fierce gunfight erupted in the East End of London between a combined force of police and army against two Latvian anarchists, following an attempted jewellery robbery, the murder of three policemen, the wounding of two others and the death of the Latvian gang's leader on 17 December.

On 3 January, police surrounded 100 Sidney Street in Stepney, where anarchists Fritz Svaars and William Sokoloff were holed up in the first-floor flat of Mrs Betsy Gershon, Sokoloff's mistress. A firefight ensued and the police, finding themselves outgunned, called in the army.

The spectacle was witnessed by a crowd of hundreds, dozens of reporters and, with the cameras of Pathé News on the scene, was the first siege in Britain to be captured on film. Controversially, footage revealed a top-hatted gentleman wearing an Astrakhan overcoat observing proceedings from the police line, and appearing to issue commands.

After several hours the house caught fire and Sokoloff, appearing at one of the upper floor windows, was shot by a marksman. Police refused to allow attending firefighters to extinguish the blaze, a decision backed up by Mr Churchill, the Home Secretary. When they eventually gained admittance, five firefighters were injured when a wall collapsed.

The case raises questions about the Liberal Party's immigration policy that has allowed an influx from Russia, and Churchill will reportedly propose a bill tightening the Aliens Act – although this may not become law.

The inadequacy of the police's firepower has also been highlighted. This is set to lead to the introduction of the Webley & Scott .32 calibre MP semi-automatic pistol to the Metropolitan Police.

CHURCHILL

58

graphic

Price 1d

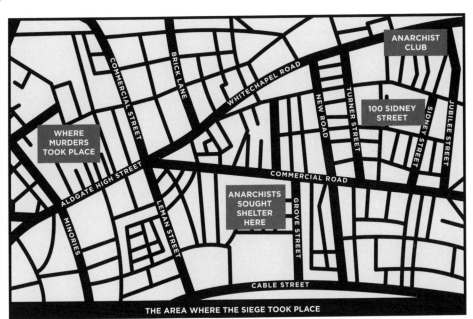

ANARCHIST CLUB

COMMERCIAL STREET

BRICK LANE

WHITECHAPEL ROAD

NEW ROAD

TURNER STREET

100 SIDNEY STREET

SIDNEY STREET

JUBILEE STREET

WHERE MURDERS TOOK PLACE

ALDGATE HIGH STREET

COMMERCIAL ROAD

LEMAN STREET

MINORIES

ANARCHISTS SOUGHT SHELTER HERE

GROVE STREET

CABLE STREET

THE AREA WHERE THE SIEGE TOOK PLACE

"I NOW INTERVENED TO SETTLE THIS DISPUTE, AT ONE MOMENT QUITE HEATED. I TOLD THE FIRE-BRIGADE OFFICER ON MY AUTHORITY AS HOME SECRETARY THAT THE HOUSE WAS TO BE ALLOWED TO BURN DOWN AND THAT HE WAS TO STAND BY IN READINESS TO PREVENT THE CONFLAGRATION FROM SPREADING."

—**Winston Churchill, in *Thoughts and Adventures*, 1932**

MAUSER AUTOMATIC PISTOL
Used by the anarchists, the pistol was capable of rapid fire. Winston Churchill had previously used the Mauser C96 in the Sudan and packed it when he travelled to South Africa in 1899, so was aware of its capabilities.

WORK

CHURCHILL'S FOLLY

**GALLIPOLI
25 APRIL 1915–
9 JANUARY 1916**

Churchill, as First Lord of the Admiralty, put forward a plan to launch a naval attack on the Ottoman capital of Constantinople (modern Istanbul), to secure the strategic 38-mile (60km) Dardanelles Strait that divided Europe and Asia. An underestimation of Ottoman troop strength, and being supplied fewer British troops than Churchill had requested from the War Office, resulted in the attack on the Gallipoli peninsula, and its subsequent land invasion with members of the Australian and New Zealand Army Corps (ANZAC), being decisively repelled. After nine months' of ferocious fighting, with devastating casualties on both sides, the invading force withdrew to Egypt.

SCAPEGOAT

Churchill had not been solely responsible for the Gallipoli fiasco, but he was credited with much of the blame. The backlash cast the government into turmoil, and prime minister Herbert Asquith's Liberals were obliged to form a coalition with the Conservatives. Churchill was sidelined in cabinet as a condition of the merger, and in 1915 resigned and headed for the front line in France as an infantry officer. He would not return to politics until 1917.

BRITISH EMPIRE
Number of killed, wounded, missing and prisoners of war:

205,000

FRANCE
Number of killed, wounded, missing and prisoners of war:

47,000

OTTOMAN EMPIRE
Number of killed, wounded, missing and prisoners of war:

251,309

108,843 TOTAL FATALITIES

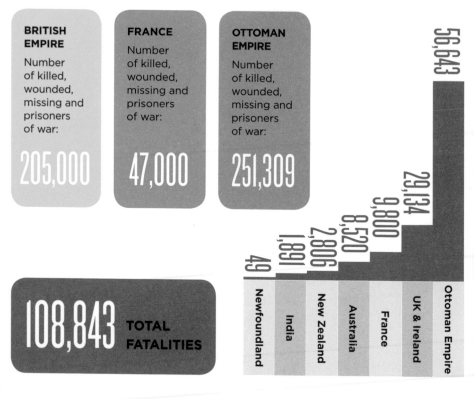

Newfoundland	India	New Zealand	Australia	France	UK & Ireland	Ottoman Empire
49	1,891	2,806	8,520	9,800	29,134	56,643

KEY

 Area occupied by 6 May

Area occupied by 4 June

Area occupied
6 August–20 December
(Suvla-Anzac Forces)

★ Major fortifications

▲◆ Forts & batteries

////// Minefield

TURKEY

BULAIR

T U R K E Y

GALLIPOLI ★

BOGHALI

D A R D A N E L L E S

MAIDOS

CANAKKALE

THE RIGHT MAN FOR THE JOB

Emerging from the 'wilderness' in the 1930s, Churchill's speeches and press articles revealed his strong convictions that, at the time, were considered extreme and were largely unheeded by those in power. But when he was enlisted as prime minister midway through the Second World War, his unstinting energy, boundless courage and singlemindedness were qualities that would inspire the embattled nation in its desperate fight against the Nazi menace.

1936

In June, King Edward VIII intends to marry American socialite Wallis Simpson, without approval of the government or the people, which would result in abdication. Churchill advises against the marriage, but supports the king. His reputation is tarnished.

1934

In a speech on defence on 7 February, he advocates that the Royal Air Force be rebuilt and a Ministry of Defence created.

1939

On 3 September, the day Britain declares war on Germany, Churchill is again appointed First Lord of the Admiralty, as part of prime minister Neville Chamberlain's War Cabinet.

Daily Post

GREAT BRITAIN DECLARES WAR ON GERMANY

1930

Although out of office, Churchill is still outspoken against home rule for India and strongly opposes Gandhi's peaceful disobedience revolt that had surfaced in the 1920s. He reportedly favours letting Gandhi die if he goes on hunger strike.

1933

He is a founder of the India Defence League, a pressure group dedicated to keeping India within the British Empire, forecasting widespread unemployment in Britain and civil strife in India if independence is granted.

INDIA

1931

Churchill warns of the dangers of Germany's rearmament.

1940

On 10 May, the day of the German invasion of France and the low countries, Chamberlain resigns as prime minister and King George VI asks Churchill, at the age of 65, to take his place at the head of a coalition government.

After the French surrender on 22 June, Churchill and a majority of his cabinet refuse to consider an armistice with Germany and he prepares the nation for a long war.

WINSTON CHURCHILL

ORATORY STYLE

- CORRECT DICTION
- RHYTHM
- ACCUMULATION OF ARGUMENT
- ANALOGY
- EXTRAVAGANT VERBAL FLOURISH

POLITICS

- GOVERNMENT MINISTER/PARTY LEADER
- HIGHEST OFFICE: PRIME MINISTER

9 YEARS AS PRIME MINISTER
(1940–45; 1951–55)

6 YEARS AS MINISTER OF DEFENCE
(1940–45; 1951–52)

90

BORN 1874 / DIED 1965

£1.8M
PRICE PAID FOR ONE
OF HIS PAINTINGS
IN 2014

43
BOOKS AUTHORED

ADOLF HITLER

On opposing sides of the Second World War, Winston Churchill and Adolf Hitler both possessed the ability to hold vast audiences spellbound with carefully sculpted speeches. But how similar were their methods of delivery?

POLITICS

- NAZI PARTY (NATIONAL SOCIALIST GERMAN WORKERS PARTY/NSDAP)
- HIGHEST OFFICE: FÜHRER AND REICH CHANCELLOR OF THE GERMAN PEOPLE

11 YEARS AS FÜHRER (1934–45)

12 YEARS AS REICH CHANCELLOR (1933–45)

ORATORY STYLE

- EXTRAVAGANT GESTURES
- FULL VOCAL RANGE
- TEMPO CHANGE
- NARROW FOCUS
- EMOTION

56

BORN 1889 / DIED 1945

$450,000
PRICE PAID FOR A COLLECTION OF HIS PAINTINGS IN 2015

2
BOOKS AUTHORED

THE BATTLE OF BRITAIN

**10 JULY–
31 OCTOBER 1940**

The Battle of Britain was given its name almost a month before it started when Winston Churchill delivered a speech in the House of Commons. On 18 June 1940, he stated "... The battle of France is over. The battle of Britain is about to begin. Upon this battle depends the survival of Christian civilization. Upon it depends our own British life and the long continuity of our institutions and our Empire. The whole fury and might of the enemy must very soon be turned on us. Hitler knows that he will have to break us in this island or lose the war. If we can stand up to him, all Europe may be free and the life of the world may move forward into broad, sunlit uplands. But if we fail, then the whole world, including the United States, including all that we have known and cared for, will sink into the abyss of a new Dark Age made more sinister, and perhaps more protracted, by the lights of perverted science. Let us therefore brace ourselves to our duties, and so bear ourselves that, if the British Empire and its Commonwealth last for a thousand years, men will still say, 'This was their finest hour'."

"NEVER IN THE FIELD OF HUMAN CONFLICT WAS SO MUCH OWED BY SO MANY TO SO FEW."

—Churchill, on exiting No. 11 Group's underground bunker at RAF Uxbridge on 16 August 1940

595 PILOTS

were from the British Dominions, and occupied European or neutral countries.

NEARLY **3,000** TOTAL AIRCREW

AVERAGE AGE **20**

AIRCRAFT FLOWN IN THE 4 MONTHS OF THE BATTLE OF BRITAIN:

= 40 planes

LUFTWAFFE 2,600

RAF 1,960

AIRCREW KILLED:

2,500

1,500

40,000 CIVILIANS KILLED

AIRCRAFT LOST:

1,977

1,744

1942 EUROPE WAS UNDER THE SHADOW OF THE SWASTIKA

Only Britain and Russia were holding out against the Nazis. The United States had entered the conflict and Churchill was involved in secret talks with Roosevelt and Stalin to coordinate a joint initiative to crush the Nazi onslaught. To do this Churchill travelled extensively.

Under the noses of the Nazis, Churchill – using the alias 'Colonel Warden' – notched up an unprecedented amount of diplomatic travel during the Second World War, not only the dozen cross-channel excursions he made to bolster French morale, but also conferences in Moscow, Malta, Newfoundland, Yalta, Quebec, Casablanca, Cairo, Tehran, Argentina and Washington. He travelled by British battleship or flew in a modified B-24 Liberator bomber and later a modified Avro Lancaster bomber.

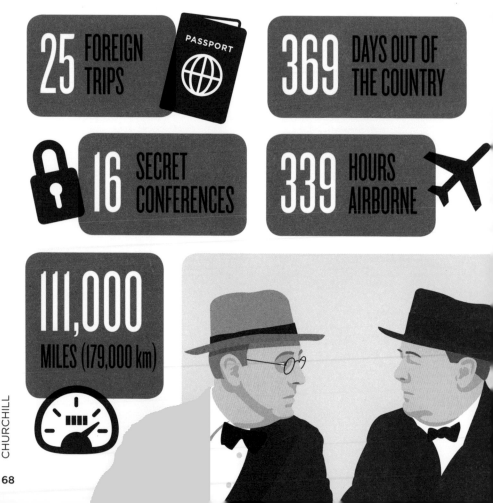

25 FOREIGN TRIPS   PASSPORT

369 DAYS OUT OF THE COUNTRY

16 SECRET CONFERENCES

339 HOURS AIRBORNE

111,000 MILES (179,000 km)

NEUTRAL

FREE

THE SPECIAL RELATIONSHIP

The oft-quoted 'special relationship' between Great Britain and the United States is not a modern alliance, but had existed in the 19th century. However, it was exemplified during the Second World War by the close friendship that was shared by Winston Churchill and president Franklin D. Roosevelt. The two leaders had first corresponded as early as 1940, but in 1941, after the US had entered the conflict in the wake of the Japanese attack on Pearl Harbor, they began a series of conferences to plot a joint strategy to defeat the Axis forces.

1940–45

1,700 LETTERS & TELEGRAMS

25 SECRET MEETINGS

WORK

THE LION'S ROAR

Churchill's stirring wartime speeches and radio broadcasts offered words of optimism to rally the troops at war and the people who remained to defend their beleaguered island in the darkest days of the Second World War.

1 BLOOD, TOIL, TEARS AND SWEAT 13 MAY 1940

In his first speech as prime minister, Churchill stated that the fight against the Nazis would determine the very survival of Britain itself.

Key lines:

"I have nothing to offer but blood, toil, tears and sweat. We have before us an ordeal of the most grievous kind. We have before us many, many long months of struggle and of suffering. You ask, what is our policy? I will say: It is to wage war, by sea, land and air, with all our might and with all the strength that God can give us."

2 WE SHALL FIGHT ON THE BEACHES 4 JUNE 1940

Speaking after evacuation of the British Expeditionary Force from Dunkirk, Churchill warned of a possible invasion of Britain by Nazi Germany and reiterated that Britain would fight on, alone if necessary.

Key lines:

"... we shall fight on the seas and oceans, we shall fight with growing confidence and growing strength in the air, we shall defend our island, whatever the cost may be, we shall fight on the beaches, we shall fight on the landing grounds, we shall fight in the fields and in the streets, we shall fight in the hills; we shall never surrender."

3 THIS WAS THEIR FINEST HOUR 18 JUNE 1940

Two days after France had sought an armistice with Germany, Churchill warned that should Britain fail to repel the Nazis the whole world would suffer.

Key lines:
"But if we fail, then the whole world ... including all that we have known and cared for, will sink into the abyss of a new Dark Age ... Let us therefore brace ourselves to our duties, and so bear ourselves that, if the British Empire and its Commonwealth last for a thousand years, men will still say, 'This was their finest hour'."

4 THE FEW 20 AUGUST 1940

Churchill's speech refers to the ongoing efforts of the Royal Air Force crews who were in the midst of fighting the Battle of Britain.

Key lines:
"The gratitude of every home in our Island, in our Empire, and indeed throughout the world, except in the abodes of the guilty, goes out to the British airmen who, undaunted by odds, unwearied in their constant challenge and mortal danger, are turning the tide of the world war by their prowess and by their devotion."

5 GIVE US THE TOOLS 9 FEBRUARY 1941

Churchill's radio broadcast, aimed at the domestic market, was also an international plea, warning of the Nazi threat to the Balkans and Russia. He appeals to the United States, who were approving the Lend Lease Act, to provide military aid to Britain.

Key lines:
"Put your confidence in us. Give us your faith and your blessing, and, under Providence, all will be well. We shall not fail or falter; we shall not weaken or tire. Neither the sudden shock of battle, nor the long-drawn trials of vigilance and exertion will wear us down. Give us the tools, and we will finish the job."

CHURCHILL VENN

Three main areas of influence combined to dictate Winston Churchill's personality and actions throughout his life and career:

ARISTOCRACY

First was the aristocratic world into which he was born, where people shared expectations about lifestyle, moral code and a certain standard of living. But a privileged upbringing does not necessarily deliver wealth.

In adult life, his beloved wife Clementine, and their children, provided the solid backbone of home life that he cherished as respite from the pressures of his responsibilities to the nation. Churchill cultivated an image that was immediately recognizable – from the famous V-salute to the ever-present cigar and a wardrobe of flamboyant clothes – even down to the way he spoke with a distinctive lisp.

ART & LITERATURE

Ambitious from a young age, Winston realized that his exquisite command of the English language, his self-taught knowledge of history, politics, literature and art could, channelled through his writing, earn him a considerable fortune.

POLITICS

Winston's father, who died quite young, was respected for his political wisdom and for learning from success and failure, while his mother – although at times distant from her son – was instrumental in coaxing him along the path of his career.

All these elements, coupled with his dogmatism and unabashed self-promotion, fuelled his rise through the ranks of the House of Commons to the pinnacle of British political life, as prime minister. His patriotism and sense of heroism coupled with an uncompromising refusal to give in, despite all odds, was grasped by the beleaguered people of Britain during the Second World War as encouragement to triumph.

POLITICS

AMBITION
POWER
TRADE UNIONISM
LIBERALISM

ART & LITERATURE

RHETORIC
DOGMATISM
WAR CORRESPONDENCE
EDWARD GIBBON
THOMAS MACAULEY

HISTORY
GENEALOGY
POETRY
AUTODIDACTISM
SHAKESPEARE
THE BIBLE

WAR
DANGER
PATRIOTISM
HEROISM
NO COMPROMISE
LORD RANDOLPH
CHURCHILL

MONEY
WRITING
PAINTING

ARISTOCRACY

CLOTHES / IMAGE
ALCOHOL / CIGARS
PROPERTY
WIFE & CHILDREN
LADY RANDOLPH
CHURCHILL

THE IRON CURTAIN

5 MARCH 1946

> "FROM STETTIN IN THE BALTIC TO TRIESTE IN THE ADRIATIC, AN IRON CURTAIN HAS DESCENDED ACROSS THE CONTINENT. BEHIND THAT LINE LIE ALL THE CAPITALS OF THE ANCIENT STATES OF CENTRAL AND EASTERN EUROPE. WARSAW, BERLIN, PRAGUE, VIENNA, BUDAPEST, BELGRADE, BUCHAREST AND SOFIA, ALL THESE FAMOUS CITIES AND THE POPULATIONS AROUND THEM LIE IN WHAT I MUST CALL THE SOVIET SPHERE."

—Winston Churchill, in a speech at Westminster College in Fulton, Missouri, 5 March 1946

In March 1946, Churchill – no longer prime minister after defeat in the 1945 general election – travelled to Fulton, Missouri, in the United States to speak at Westminster College campus. His speech, 'The Sinews of Peace', presented the Western bloc's attitudes towards the Eastern bloc, and is widely regarded as the first shot in the Cold War, which did not end until 1991. Sharing the platform with Harry S. Truman, who succeeded Roosevelt as president after his death in April 1945, Churchill emphasized the need to maintain close ties between Great Britain and the United States and to prevent the spread of communism.

In this landmark speech, he referred to an "iron curtain". This was a term originally applied to fireproof curtains in theatres, but Churchill adopted it as the name for the metaphorical boundary that divided Europe after the Second World War, which was epitomized by the Berlin Wall and other border defences.

STALIN'S REACTION

Churchill's reference to the distrust the Allied Nations felt towards the Soviet Union at the end of the Second World War angered its leader, Joseph Stalin, who considered the speech to be 'war mongering'.

BERLIN

COMMUNIS STATES

NATO COUNTRIES

IRON CURTAIN

04
LEGACY

"REMEMBER HIM, FOR HE SAVED ALL OF YOU: PUDGY AND NOT VERY LARGE BUT SOMEHOW MASSIVE AND INDOMITABLE; BABY-FACED, WITH SNUB NOSE, SQUARE CHIN, RHEUMY EYES ON OCCASION GIVEN TO TEARS; A THWARTED ACTOR'S TASTE FOR CLOTHES THAT WOULD HAVE LOOKED RIDICULOUS ON A LESS SPLENDID MAN ..."

—C.L. Sulzberger, in his book *The American Heritage Picture History of World War II*, 1966

CHURCHILL

OPERATION HOPE NOT

'Operation Hope Not' was the codename for Churchill's grand state funeral, which had been sanctioned by royal decree. Such an honour was rare for a British civilian, but considered to be commensurate with the statesman's decisive role in history.

90 cannon shots were fired from Hyde Park, each one marking a year of Churchill's life

12 YEARS PLANNING

After his stroke in 1953, the government began making plans for his state funeral.

350 million people across the globe watched on television

LYING IN STATE

Churchill lay in state in Westminster Hall from 27 January until the funeral service on 30 January.

THE PROCESSION ROUTE

300,000 MOURNERS FILED PAST HIS COFFIN

ALDWYCH

THE STRAND

VICTORIA EMBANKMENT

WATERLOO BRI

FESTIVAL HALL PIER

THE FUNERAL SERVICE

Big Ben chimed at 9:45am to mark the start of the lavish funeral service, and was silent for the remainder of the day.

WHITEHALL

WATERLOO STATIO

START

WESTMINSTER HALL

The main church service was held in St Paul's Cathedral, attended by ...

GOVERNMENT OFFICIALS
6 MONARCHS
6 PRESIDENTS
16 PRIME MINISTERS
112 NATIONS REPRESENTED
THE QUEEN AND MEMBERS OF THE ROYAL HOUSEHOLD

1 MILLION

people lined the route of the funeral procession

Transferred to the MV *Havengore*, the casket was then transported up the River Thames to Festival Hall Pier beneath a fly-by of 16 Royal Air Force fighter jets, while shipping cranes were bowed on the banks.

ST PAUL'S

FLEET STREET

THREADNEEDLE STREET

CANNON ST

EAST CHEAP

BLACKFRIARS BRIDGE

SOUTHWARK BRIDGE

LONDON BRIDGE

MFORD STREET

BLACKFRIARS ROAD

FINISH

At Waterloo station, the casket was transferred to a specially prepared carriage as part of a funeral train of Pullman coaches carrying family mourners. It was then hauled by the Battle of Britain class steam locomotive No. 21C151 *Winston Churchill* to Oxfordshire, where Winston was interred in St Martin's Churchyard, in a private family ceremony.

TMINSTER BRIDGE RD

CHURCHILL WAR ROOMS
WHITEHALL, LONDON

During the Second World War, the nerve centre of Britain's war effort was located deep within a reinforced basement in Whitehall. The Cabinet War Rooms provided a safe working space for members of the government and military strategists.

ST. JAMES'S PARK

SECRET BUNKER

The bunker was created in 1938 beneath the New Public Offices building, near Parliament Square. The building, which now accommodates HM Treasury, had a strong steel frame and capacious basement. Communications and broadcasting equipment, sound-proofing, ventilation and reinforcement were installed. Meeting rooms for the War Cabinet during air raids, as well as a map room for military intelligence, were also constructed.

115 WAR CABINET MEETINGS

WAR CABINET ROOM

CHURCHILL'S OFFICE-BEDROOM

COMMUNICATIONS ROOM

THE SLAB

During the Blitz in October 1940, a 5 feet (1.5 m) thick layer of concrete was constructed above the Cabinet War Rooms to further protect the bunker against bomb damage. 'The Slab' was subsequently extended, allowing more facilities to be installed within the complex.

CHURCHILL MUSEUM

Now a museum, the War Rooms contain: 9,000 square feet (850 m²) of biographical material, a 50 foot (15 m) interactive table with access to digitized material from the Churchill Archives Centre, Cambridge, extracts from wartime speeches, letters exchanged between Churchill and his wife and many objects relating to all periods of his life.

The Imperial War Museum opened the doors of the War Rooms to the public in 1984. They now receive more than ...

300,000 VISITORS A YEAR

CHIEF OF STAFF CONFERENCE ROOM

CHURCHILL'S KITCHEN

Lights in the map room were switched off for the first time in six years on 16 August 1945.

MAP ROOM

BBC BROADCASTING ROOM

CHURCHILL'S HOUSE & GARDENS: CHARTWELL, WESTERHAM, KENT

Just 2 miles (3 km) south of Westerham, Kent, lies Chartwell – the much-loved home of Winston and Clementine Churchill, purchased in 1922 and where they remained until his death.

Set within 80 acres (32 ha) of farmland and woodland, the red-brick farmhouse had been enlarged during the 19th century in a Victorian style. Churchill had been entranced by the view, a spectacular panorama across the Weald of Kent. In the 1920s architect Philip Tilden modernized and extended the property in a more sympathetic vernacular.

In 1946, Sir Winston – at the age of 72 – and Lady Clementine found maintaining the large estate a drain on their resources. A solution was found by newspaper publisher Lord Camrose and a consortium of 10 wealthy businessmen. Each donated £5,000 to purchase the property, allowing the couple to continue to live there, with the proviso that the estate was presented to the nation on their deaths. However, on Sir Winston's death, Clementine offered it to the National Trust, who opened it to the public in 1966.

The rooms of the house remain decorated and furnished much as they were when the family lived there, with the addition of memorabilia and a display of Churchill's many honours and medals.

Terraced grounds with lawns and mixed herbaceous gardens descend to lakes created by Winston, a water garden and Lady Churchill's rose garden. They also feature a kitchen garden and the Marycot, a playhouse created for the couple's youngest daughter Mary.

UNITED KINGDOM

WESTERHAM

KEY

Main house

Studio

The wall
Winston built

Golden Orfe pond

Pet graves

Croquet lawn

Urn island

Kitchen garden

Golden rose
avenue

Lady Churchill's
rose garden

FICTION AND FABLE

Whether portrayed by some of the finest actors of the day in war movies or theatrical performances, risen from the grave into a dystopian world, paraphrased by a 1960s rock band or battling the Daleks in a science-fiction adventure romp, Winston Churchill's cigar-puffing icon of the British fighting spirit has been immortalized in numerous fictional works since he first burst onto the political stage.

ROYAL PASTICHE

The first screen portrayal of Churchill was by Scottish actor C.M. Hallard in *Royal Cavalcade* (1935), a pastiche of great events during the reign of King George V.

PLAYING FOR LAUGHS

Peter Sellers portrayed Churchill in various episodes of the BBC radio comedy *The Goon Show*.

MEET THE MONARCH

Edward Fox replaced Robert Hardy's Churchill in *The Audience* (2013), which centres on the weekly meetings between Queen Elizabeth II (played by Dame Helen Mirren) and her prime ministers.

DOMINION

C.J. Sansom's novel *Dominion* (2012) is a political thriller set in the early 1950s in which Churchill did not become prime minister in 1940, and Britain surrenders to Nazi Germany. Churchill leads a resistance group responsible for daubing V signs in public places.

THE VOICE

Richard Burton voiced extracts from Churchill's memoirs in 26 episodes of the documentary *The Valiant Years* (1960–3), and played him in the biopic *The Gathering Storm* (1974).

IN THE CHARTS

The Kinks recorded 'Mr Churchill Says' for their 1969 album *Arthur (Or the Decline and Fall of the British Empire)*, whose lyrics paraphrase parts of several famous Churchill speeches.

GAMER

Video game, *Assassin's Creed Syndicate*, features Churchill helping to defend London in the First World War.

PORTRAYED IN:

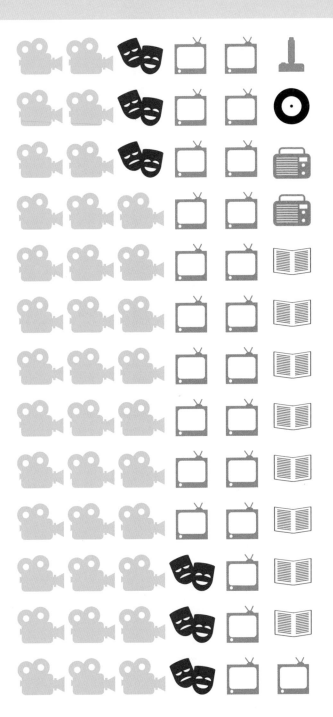

36 FILMS

6 PLAYS

24 TV SHOWS

8 BOOKS

2 RADIO SHOWS

1 SONG

1 COMPUTER GAME

IN HIS NAME

Churchill's name has been immortalized across the world in innumerable objects. Edifices, roads, avenues, squares, streets, parks, stations, boulevards, neighbourhoods and public buildings – even a large dock in the port of Antwerp, Belgium – have been christened in his honour.

BIG SMOKE

Winston's preferred brand of cigar was the Cuban Romeo y Julieta, whose manufacturer created one of its vitolas in his honour. 'Churchill' cigars – named due to the size and shape – are also now produced by various manufacturers in a range of variants.

SHIPSHAPE

Despite the common use of feminine pronouns when referring to ships, various sailing craft were named for Churchill:

ROYAL NAVY WARSHIP HMS *CHURCHILL* Originally USS *Herndon* (1940–4)

NUCLEAR POWERED CHURCHILL-CLASS FLEET SUBMARINE HMS *CHURCHILL* (1970–91)

DESTROYER USS *WINSTON S. CHURCHILL* OF THE UNITED STATES NAVY (1999–)

WINSTON CHURCHILL

21C

VINTAGE CUVÉE

Pol Roger was Winston's favourite Champagne. Following his death in 1965, a black border was added to the label of bottles shipped to the UK as a sign of mourning, a feature that was not lifted until 1990. In 1984, the first prestige vintage *Cuvée Sir Winston Churchill 1975* was launched at Blenheim.

HIGHEST HONOUR

The Churchill Mountains, a range of 13 peaks in Antarctica, borders the western side of the Ross Ice Shelf between Byrd Glacier and Nimrod Glacier.

HIGHEST SUMMIT:
MOUNT ALBERT MARKHAM

10,515 feet (3,205 m)

Winston was honoured with a mountain range in the Canadian Rockies and Mount Churchill in Eastern Alaska.

DANISH CAR FERRY MS *WINSTON CHURCHILL* **(1967–2004)**

Churchill has also lent his name to a cargo ship and a lighthouse tender.

SAIL TRAINING SCHOONER *SIR WINSTON CHURCHILL,* built in 1966

FIRST CLASS

In 1947, Southern Railway named their Battle of Britain class 4-6-2 *Pacific* steam locomotive No. 21C151 after the great man, in a ceremony at Waterloo station. Invited to name the locomotive, Churchill declined, citing a prior engagement. The loco, built at Brighton Works in 1946, was later used to haul Churchill's funeral train. It is now preserved at the National Railway Museum, York.

SOUTHERN

LEGACY

WINSTON'S WORDS

8 – 10 MILLION WORDS

64 YEARS

Churchill received the Nobel Prize for Literature in 1953 "for his mastery of historical and biographical description as well as for brilliant oratory in defending exalted human values". Although there are innumerable book editions of Churchill's writings compiled by independent editors, and countless tomes written about the great statesman by other authors, up until the time of his death, Churchill could boast an impressive output:

31 NON-FICTION BOOKS

INCLUDING **5** MAJOR VOLUMES

16,151 PAGES

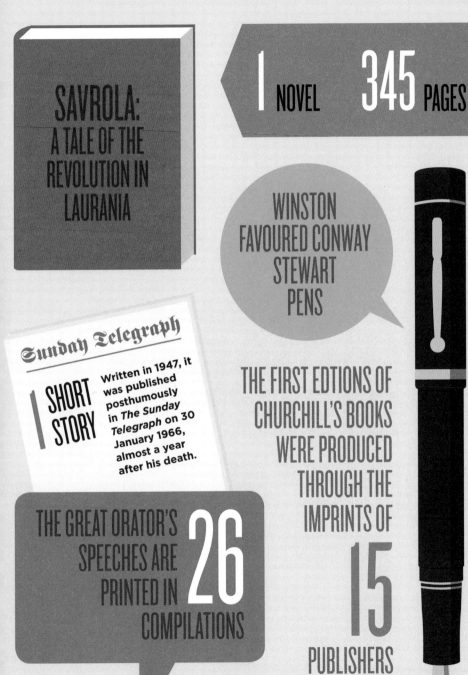

SAVROLA:
A TALE OF THE
REVOLUTION IN
LAURANIA

1 NOVEL   345 PAGES

WINSTON
FAVOURED CONWAY
STEWART
PENS

Sunday Telegraph

1 SHORT
STORY

Written in 1947, it
was published
posthumously
in *The Sunday
Telegraph* on 30
January 1966,
almost a year
after his death.

THE FIRST EDTIONS OF
CHURCHILL'S BOOKS
WERE PRODUCED
THROUGH THE
IMPRINTS OF
15
PUBLISHERS

THE GREAT ORATOR'S
SPEECHES ARE
PRINTED IN
26
COMPILATIONS

TYPOGRAPHIC CHURCHILL

orator

"We Shall Fight on the Beaches"

Second World War

cigars

onesie

V for Victory!

polo

Winston

The Few

black dog

lisp

Cuba

Sandhurst

Blitz

alcohol

Chartwell

Gallipoli

mouthwash

literature

Sidney Street siege

Hussar

Commonwealth

"Special Relationship"

Clementine

whisky

Blenheim Palace

politics

prisoner of war

prime minister

rhetoric

Roosevelt

British Empire

Churchill

Boer War

Homburg

war correspondence

North-West frontier

dogmatic

gambling

Champagne

Dardanelles

Woom

bricklaying

Woodstock

Battle of Britain

"Never Give In!"

finest hour

BIOGRAPHIES

**Sir Max Aitken
(1879–1964)**
Canadian businessman, politician and newspaper proprietor who held numerous parliamentary offices in the First World War. He was appointed Minister for Aircraft Production by Churchill during the Second World War.

**Brendan Bracken
(1901–58)**
Irish-born businessman and minister in the Conservative cabinet. Supported Churchill in the Second World War. Served as Minister of Information in 1941–5, and his business interests included founding the modern *Financial Times* and publishing *The Economist*.

**Elizabeth Ann Everest
(c. 1832–95)**
Winston's childhood nanny was effectively his surrogate mother, since his parents were both active in society, and somewhat distant. 'Woom', as she was affectionately known, remained with the family for 18 years.

**Frederick Lindemann
(1886–1957)**
English physicist who met Winston in the 1920s in a charity tennis match. Churchill appointed him leading scientific adviser to the government during the Second World War, and they met almost daily for the duration of the conflict.

**John Strange Spencer-Churchill
(1880–1947)**
Winston's younger brother 'Jack' was born in Dublin. He served in the South African Light Horse alongside war correspondent Winston during the Boer War, and was a major in the First World War.

**Lord Randolph Spencer-Churchill
(1849–95)**
A charismatic and influential Conservative Party figure, Winston's father was Leader of the House of Commons and Chancellor of the Exchequer. His political career ended in resignation over demands on the Treasury.

William Bourke Cockran (1854–1923)

On his first visit to New York, US, 20-year-old Winston stayed with Cockran, a family friend. The Democratic politician and member of the House of Representatives became his first political mentor and a role model for Churchill's own approach to oratory.

Clementine Ogilvy Hozier (1885–1977)

Daughter of Henry Hozier and Lady Blanche Hozier. She met Winston in 1904 and they were reacquainted in 1908. After corresponding for some months, she accepted his proposal, they were married and had five children.

Frederick Edwin Smith (1872–1930)

British Conservative politician and barrister. He was one of Churchill's closest personal and political friends. He served as Solicitor General and Attorney General, becoming Lord Chancellor in Lloyd George's government, aged only 47.

Franklin D. Roosevelt (1882–1945)

The 32nd President of the United States had a close relationship with Winston Churchill during the Second World War, working with him, the Soviet leader Joseph Stalin and the Chinese military leader Chiang Kai-shek to defeat the Axis powers.

Jeanette 'Jennie' Jerome (1854–1921)

Churchill's mother was born in New York. A great beauty, she married Lord Randolph Churchill in 1874. Winston adored her and her contacts assisted his career. After Randolph's death, she remarried twice.

Paul Maze (1887–1979)

An Anglo-French Post-Impressionist painter, known for his depiction of quintessentially English scenes, Maze met Winston in the First World War trenches and the pair became lifelong friends. Maze tutored Winston in drawing and painting techniques.

friend

family

mentor

childhood influence

INDEX

CHURCHILL

WINSTON SMOKED UP TO 70 CIGARS EVERY WEEK

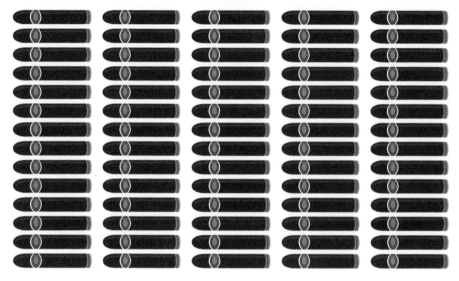